The

Model way of Getting Riches

The secret book of Riches

By

David J. Steel

Copyright ©

Table of contents:

Preface:

This book is sober-minded, not philosophical; it is a down-to-earth manual, not a composition of hypotheses. It is expected for the people whose most squeezing need is for cash; who wish to get rich first, and philosophize subsequently. It is for the individuals who have, up until this point, carved out neither the opportunity, the means, nor the valuable chance to go profoundly into the investigation of transcendentalism, however, who need results and who will accept the decisions of science as a reason for the activity, without going into every one of the cycles by which those ends were reached. Normally, the peruser will take the central assertions upon confidence, similarly as he would take proclamations concerning a law of electrical activity assuming that they were proclaimed by a Marconi or an Edison; and, taking the explanations upon confidence, that he will demonstrate their reality by following up on them without dread or wavering. Each man or lady who does this will positively get rich; for the science thus applied is a careful science, and disappointment is unimaginable. For the advantage, notwithstanding, of the people who wish to explore philosophical speculations and thus secure a legitimate reason for confidence, I will here refer to specific specialists. The monistic hypothesis of the universe - the hypothesis that One is All, and that Everything is One, that one Substance shows itself as appearing to be numerous components of the material world - is of Hindu beginning, and has been continuously winning its direction into the possibility of the western world for 200 years.

It is the support of the huge number of Oriental perspectives, and of those of Descartes, Spinoza, Leibnitz, Schopenhauer, Hegel, and Emerson.

The peruser who might dig into the philosophical groundwork of this is encouraged to understand Hegel and Emerson for himself. Recorded as a hard copy of this book I have forfeited any remaining contemplations to conventionality and effortlessness of style so that all could comprehend. The strategy set down thus was found from the finishes of reasoning; it has been completely tried, and bears the preeminent trial of pragmatic investigation; it works. On the off chance that you wish to know how the ends were shown up, read the compositions of the writers referenced above; and assuming that you wish to procure the products of their ways of thinking in genuine practice, read this book and do precisely as it advises you to do.

Chapter. 1

The Option To Be Rich:

Anything that might be said in recognition of destitution, the reality stays that it is preposterous to expect to carry on with a truly complete or effective life except if one is rich. Without a lot of money, no man can develop his abilities or reach their highest possible degree. This is because in order to unleash the spirit and foster ability, a person needs a variety of resources to use, which they cannot get without the money to do so.

A man creates at the top of the priority list, soul, and body by utilizing things, and society is coordinated to the point that man should have the cash to turn into the owner of things; thus, the premise of all progression for man should be the study of getting rich. The object of all life is advancement, and all that lives have a basic right to all the improvement it is fit for achieving. Man's on the whole correct to live implies his entitlement to have the free and unhindered

utilization of the multitude of things that might be important to his fullest mental, profound, and actual unfoldment; or, all in all, his entitlement to be rich. In this book, I will not discuss wealth in a metaphorical manner; to be truly rich doesn't mean to be fulfilled or happy with a bit. No man should be happy with a tad if he is equipped for utilizing and getting a charge out of something else. The reason for Nature is the progression and unfoldment of life; and each man ought to have all that can add to the influence; class, excellence, and lavishness of life; to be happy with less is wicked. The one who claims all he needs for the living of all the daily routine he is equipped for experiencing is rich, and
all he needs is a lot of money
. Life has progressed up until this point, and become so perplexing, that even the most conventional man or lady requires a lot of abundance to live in a way that even methodologies culminate. Each individual normally needs to turn out to be all that they are fit for turning into; this longing to acknowledge natural prospects is innate in human instinct; we

can't resist the urge to need to be everything that could have been. Outcome throughout everyday life

is becoming what you need to be; you can become what you need to be exclusively by utilizing things, and you can have the free utilization of things just as you become rich enough to get them. To comprehend the study of getting rich is thus the most fundamental of all information. There is nothing out of sorts in needing to get rich. The longing for wealth is actually the craving for a more extravagant, more full, and more bountiful life; and that want is acclaim commendable. The one who doesn't want to live more plentifully is unusual, thus the one who doesn't want to have the cash to the point of purchasing all he needs is strange. There are three thought processes in which we live; we live for the body, we live for the psyche, and we live for the spirit. None of these is preferable or holier than the other; all are similarly attractive, and nobody of the three - - body, psyche, or soul - - can live completely if both of the others are stopped from full life and articulation. There's something wrong with it or honorable to live just for the spirit and deny the brain or body; it is inappropriate to live for the insight and deny the body or soul. We are undeniably familiar with the odious results of living for the body and denying both psyche and soul; and we see that the genuine method is the total articulation of everything that could be given forward through body, brain, and soul. Anything that he can say, no man can be truly cheerful or fulfilled except if his body is living completely in each capability, and except if the equivalent is valid for his brain and his spirit. In any place where there is an unexpressed chance, or capability not performed, there is unsatisfied craving. Want is plausibility looking for articulation, or capability looking for execution. Man can't live completely in the body without great food, open to attire, and a warm safe house; and without independence from unnecessary work. Rest and diversion are likewise important to his genuine life. He can't live completely as a top priority without books and time to concentrate on them, without a potential open door for movement and perception, or without scholarly friendship. To live completely as a primary concern he should have scholarly entertainment, and should encircle himself with every one of the objects of workmanship and magnificence he is equipped for utilizing and appreciating.

To live completely in the spirit, man should have endless love denied articulation by destitution. A man's most elevated satisfaction is found in the bestowal of advantages on those he cherishes; love tracks down its most regular and unconstrained articulation in giving. The one who doesn't have anything to give can't fill his place as a spouse or father, as a resident, or as a man. It is in the utilization of material things that a man tracks down full life for his body, fosters his psyche, and unfurls his spirit. It is thus of incomparable significance to him that he ought to be rich. It is entirely correct that you ought to want to be rich; assuming you are a typical man or lady you can't resist the urge to do as such. It is completely correct that you ought to focus entirely on the Study of Getting Rich, for it is the noblest and generally fundamental, everything being equal. Assuming you disregard this review, you are neglecting your obligation to yourself, to God, and humankind; for you can deliver to God and mankind no more prominent assistance than to take full advantage of yourself.

Chapter. 2

The science of being wealthy exists.

There is a precise science—like algebra or arithmetic—to becoming wealthy. Any individual can become wealthy with mathematical certainty if he learns and follows the rules that govern the process of accumulating wealth. The possession of money and property results from acting in a particular manner; individuals who act in this Particular Manner, whether on purpose or accidentally, become wealthy; No matter how hard they work or how talented they are, individuals who do not act in this Certain Way continue to live in poverty. Natural law dictates that the same causes always result in similar results, thus anyone who learns to act in this way will invariably become wealthy. The following facts demonstrate that the aforementioned claim is accurate: The environment has nothing to do with wealth because if it did, everyone in certain neighborhoods would be wealthy, everyone in one city would be wealthy while everyone in other towns would be poor, and everyone in one state would be rich while everyone in another state would be poor. But everywhere we look, we see wealthy and impoverished people coexisting in the same setting and frequently working in related fields. When two men work in the same industry and community but one becomes wealthy while the other remains in poverty, it is evident that the environment is not the primary factor in determining wealth. Even while some surroundings may be more conductive than others, when two guys working in the same industry and living in the same neighborhood succeed while the other fails, it suggests that doing things in a particular way is what leads to success. Also, many people who are talented at doing things in a certain manner are not the only ones who are

Those with considerable talent struggle to make ends meet, while those with little talent prosper. When we examine the wealthy, we discover that they are a typical group in every way, with no special skills or characteristics that set them apart from other guys. They do not get wealthy because they have skills and capabilities that other guys do not, but rather because they have a particular way of doing things. Wealth does not come through "thrift" or saving; many people who are extremely frugal are impoverished, while unrestrained spenders frequently become wealthy. Furthermore, becoming wealthy is not a result of carrying out tasks that others overlook; two businessmen will frequently carry out nearly identical tasks, but one will emerge wealthy while the other will either continue in poverty or go bankrupt. All of these facts force us to draw the conclusion that acting in a particular way leads to financial success. If achieving wealth requires acting in a certain way, and similar causes always have similar effects, then everybody who is able to act in that way has the potential to achieve wealth. and the whole matter is brought inside the domain of accurate science. Here, the concern of whether this Particular Way won't be so challenging that only a select few will choose to pursue it, arises. As we have seen in terms of inherent ability, this is not true. Rich people are born with talent, poor people are born with stupidity, the academically gifted are born with wealth, the physically fit are born with wealth, and the weak and unwell are born with wealth. But some level of intelligence and comprehension is obviously necessary, anyone with the natural capacity to read and comprehend these words can undoubtedly become wealthy. We have shown that it is not an environmental issue as well. One wouldn't go to the heart of the Sahara and expect to do good business; location matters. To get wealthy, one must deal with men and be in an environment where there are people to deal with; if these

are prone to behave in the manner that you desire, the better. But that's pretty much it in terms of the environment. You can become wealthy if anyone else in your town or state does, as well as if anyone else in your community. Once more, picking a specific business or vocation is not necessary. Individuals get wealthy in every industry and profession, while their next-door neighbors who work in the same field continue to live in poverty. It is true that you will perform at your best in a line of work that you enjoy and find agreeable; additionally, if you have well-developed abilities, you will perform at your best in a line of work that allows you to put those talents to use. A business that is appropriate for your area will also be the most successful for you. For example, an ice cream shop would perform better in a warm climate than in Greenland, and a salmon fishery would perform better in the Northwest than in Florida, where there are no salmon. Aside from these fundamental restrictions, however, becoming wealthy is more dependent on learning how to do things a certain way than it is on starting a specific firm. If you are currently in a company and someone else in your community is becoming wealthy in the same industry while you are not, it is likely because you are not carrying out your operations in the same manner. No one is prohibited from becoming wealthy due to a lack of resources. It is true that as you acquire capital, growth gets easier and more rapid; nevertheless, someone who possesses capital is already wealthy and does not need to think about how to do so. Regardless of how poor you may be, if you start acting in a certain way, you will start getting affluent and building up capital. Getting capital is a step in the process of being wealthy, and it's a component of the outcome that usually follows doing things a certain way. You may be the poorest guy on the continent, be heavily in debt, and lack friends, influence, and resources, but if you start acting in this manner, you will inevitably start becoming wealthy since similar causes must result in similar results. If you lack capital, you can acquire it; if you are in the incorrect line of work, you can change;

If you are in the wrong place, you can move to the right place by starting in your current business and location and doing things in a specific way that leads to success.

Chapter. 3

The possibility is monopolized.

Since opportunity has been denied to him and because the riches have been monopolized and enclosed by others, NO man is kept in poverty. Although you might not be able to conduct business in some areas, there are still options available to you. Very likely, it would be difficult for you to take over one of the large railroad networks; that industry is pretty much monopolized. But, the electric train industry is still young and has plenty of room for growth. It won't be long before air traffic and transportation become a significant industry that employs hundreds of thousands, if not millions, of people across all of its sectors. Instead of vying for a spot in the steam railway industry with J.J. Hill and others, why not focus on the development of aerial transportation? You indeed have very little chance of owning the factory where you work if you are a worker employed by the steel trust, but it is also true that if you start acting in a certain way, you can quickly leave the steel trust's employ. Men who live on little plots of land and cultivate them intensively now have a lot of possibilities and will undoubtedly become wealthy. You may claim that it is difficult for you to get land, but I'm going to show you that it is possible and that, if you put in the necessary effort, you can acquire a farm. The tide of opportunity flows in different directions at different times, depending on the demands of the group as a whole and the specific stage of social evolution that has been attained. It is currently pointing toward agriculture and related professions and businesses in America. Today, the manufacturing worker in his line has the opportunity. It is accessible to businessmen who supply farmers more frequently than they supply industrial workers, as well as to professionals who service farmers more frequently than they serve the working class.

The individual who will swim with the tide rather than against it will have plenty of chances. As a result, neither the factory workers individually or collectively are denied the opportunity. The masters are not "keeping down" the workers, and neither are the capital trusts and combinations "grounding" them. They as a class are where they are because they do not act in a particular manner. If American workers so desired, they might emulate their brethren in Belgium and other nations and create large department stores and cooperative enterprises; they could elect members from their own class to public office; and they could adopt laws encouraging the growth of such cooperative industries. and in a few years, they would be able to peacefully occupy the industrial area. The law of wealth is the same for them as it is for everyone else, therefore the working class can become the master class anytime they start acting in a certain way. They need to understand this because if they don't, they will stay in their current position. But, the individual worker is not constrained by his class's ignorance or mental laziness; he can ride the wave of opportunity to riches. and he will learn how from this book. A lack of wealth does not keep anyone in poverty; there is more than enough for everyone. With just the building materials produced in the United States, a palace the size of the capital building in Washington could be constructed for every family on the planet. In addition, with intensive farming, this nation could produce enough wool, cotton, linen, and silk to clothe everyone in the world in clothing as fine as Solomon wore in his heyday, along with enough food to feed them all lavishly. The unseen supply IS infinite, while the apparent supply is almost endless. One primordial material, from which all things originate, is the source of all you see in the world. Older forms fade away while new ones are continuously taking their place, yet they are all only different shapes that One Thing assumes.

The amount of Original Material, also known as Formless Matter, is infinite. It is what the cosmos is composed of, Yet not all of it went into creating the universe. The Original Material, also known as the formless Thing or the foundation of all things, permeates and fills the voids within, through, and between the forms of the visible cosmos. Even then, the supply of the universal raw material should not have been depleted; ten thousand times as much as has been produced may still be produced. As a result, neither nature nor a lack of resources may cause a guy to be impoverished. Natural resources are an endless source of wealth; there is never a shortage. Original Substance is continually developing new forms and is bursting with creative energy. When the supply of building materials runs out, more will be made; likewise, when the soil is depleted to the point where it is no longer able to support the growth of crops for food and clothes, it will be regenerated or new soil will be created. If a man is still at a point in his social evolution where he needs gold and silver after all the earth's gold and silver have been mined, more will be produced from the Formless.

Man's needs are met by the Formless Matter, which won't allow him to go without any good things. This is true of all of mankind; the race is always abundantly wealthy as a whole, and if any individuals are impoverished, it is because they do not adhere to the Particular Way of Life that makes the Individual Man Rich. The Formless Thing is thought-provoking, clever material. It is alive and constantly driven to acquire additional life. The desire to live longer is a basic instinct of life. It is also in the nature of intelligence to grow, and of consciousness to look for new ways to express itself. Formless Living Substances created the universe of forms by taking on shape in order to express themselves more fully. The universe is a huge Living Presence that is compelled to expand and become fully functional.

Nature was created to promote the spread of life; this is what drives it. Everything that might potentially promote life is abundantly provided for this reason; there can never be a shortage until God contradicts himself and undoes his own deeds. You are not kept impoverished by a lack of wealth; as I'll show a little later, even the resources of the Formless Supply are at the beck and call of anyone who is willing to act and think in a particular way.

Chapter 4

The Primary Guideline in The Study of Getting Rich.

Believed is the main influence which can create unmistakable wealth from the Nebulous Substance. The stuff from which everything is made is a substance that thinks, and an idea of structure in this substance creates the structure. Unique Substance moves as per its contemplations; each structure and cycle you find in nature is the noticeable articulation of an idea in Unique Substance. As the Undefined Stuff thinks about a structure, it takes that structure; as it thinks about a movement, it makes that movement. That is the way all things were made. We live in an ideal world, which is essential for an ideal universe. The possibility of a moving universe reached out all through Undefined Substance, and the Reasoning Stuff moving as indicated by that naturally suspected, appeared as frameworks of planets, and keeps up with that structure. Thinking Substance appears as its suspected, and moves as indicated by the naturally suspected.

Holding the possibility of a surrounding arrangement of suns and universes, it appears as these bodies and moves them as it naturally suspects. Thinking of the type of a sluggish developing oak tree, it moves in like manner and produces the tree, however, hundreds of years might be expected to accomplish the work. In making, the Nebulous appears to move as per the lines of movement it has laid out; the prospect of an oak tree doesn't cause the moment the development of a completely mature tree, yet it begins moving the powers which will create the tree, along laid out lines of development. Each considered structure, held in thinking Substance, causes the production of the structure, yet consistently, or possibly for the most part, along lines of development and activity previously settled. The prospect of a place of a specific development, in the event that it was put forth for Undefined Substance, probably won't cause the moment arrangement, of the house; however, it would cause the turning of imaginative energies previously working in exchange and business into such diverts as to bring about the fast structure of the house. Furthermore, in the event that there were no current channels through which the imaginative energy could work, then the house would be framed straightforwardly from the basic substance, without hanging tight for the sluggish cycles of the natural and inorganic world.

Unique Substance without causing the production of the structure. Man is a reasoning community, and can begin thinking. Every one of the structures that man styles with his hands should first exist in quite a while though; he can't shape a thing until he has imagined that thing. Thus far man has bound his endeavors entirely to craft by his hands; he has applied difficult work to the universe of structures, trying to change or adjust those generally existing. He has never considered attempting to cause the formation of new structures by putting forth his considerations for Nebulous Substance. At the point when man has a thought structure, he takes material from the types of nature and makes a picture of the structure which is to him. He has, up to this point, put forth practically zero attempts to co-work with Shapeless Insight; to work "with the Dad." He has not imagined that he can "do what he sees Dad doing." Man reshapes and adjusts existing structures through physical work; he has focused on the inquiry of whether he may not deliver things from an Indistinct Substance by imparting his contemplations to it. We propose to demonstrate that he might do as such; to demonstrate that any man or lady might do as such, and to show how.

As our initial step, we should set down three central recommendations. To start with, we affirm that there is one unique nebulous stuff, or substance, from which everything is made. Every one of the apparently numerous components is nevertheless various introductions of one component; every one of the many structures found in natural and inorganic nature is nevertheless various shapes, produced using similar stuff. Furthermore, this stuff is thinking stuff; an idea held in it delivers the type of the idea. Thought, in thinking substance, produces shapes. Man is a reasoning place, fit for unique ideas; on the off chance that man can impart his thinking to a unique reasoning substance, he can cause the creation, or development, of what he thinks about. To sum up this - - There is reasoning stuff from which everything is made, and which, in its unique state, pervades, enters, and fills the interspaces of the universe.

An idea, in this substance, delivers what is imaged by the idea. Man can shape things in his idea, and, by putting forth his thinking for amorphous substances, can cause what he thinks is going to be made. It might very well be inquired as to whether I can demonstrate these assertions; and without delving into subtleties, I answer that I can do as such, both by rationale and experience. Thinking back from the peculiarities of structure and thought, I come to one unique reasoning substance; and thinking forward from this thinking substance, I come to labor supply to cause the development of what he thinks about. What's more, by exploring, I see the thinking as valid; and this is my most grounded evidence. Assuming a small time who peruses this book gets rich by doing everything it says to him to do, that is proof on the side of my case; however, in the event that each man who does everything that it says to him to do gets rich, that is positive evidence until somebody goes through the cycle and falls flat.

The hypothesis is valid until the interaction fizzles; and this cycle won't come up short, for each man who does precisely the exact thing this book instructs him to do will get rich. I have said that men get rich by getting things done with a specific goal in mind; and to do as such, men should become ready to think with a particular goal in mind. A man's approach to doing things is the immediate consequence of the manner in which he ponders things. To get things done in a manner you believe that you should do, you should secure the capacity to think in the manner in which you need to think; this is the most vital move toward getting rich. To think what you need to believe is to think TRUTH, paying little mind to appearances. Each man has the normal and intrinsic ability to think what he needs to think, yet he expects definitely more work to do as such than it

does to think about the contemplations which are proposed by appearances. To think as indicated by appearance is simple; to think truth paying little mind to appearances is arduous and requires the use of more power than some other work man is called upon to perform. There is no work from which a great many people recoil as they do from that of supported and back-to-back thought; it is the hardest work on the planet. This is particularly evident when the truth is in opposition to appearances. Each appearance in the noticeable world will in general deliver a comparing structure in the psyche which notices it, and this must be forestalled by holding the possibility of Reality.

To view the presence of sickness will create the type of illness as far as you could tell, and at last in your body, except if you hold the possibility of reality, which is that there is no infection; it is just an appearance, and actually wellbeing. To view the appearances of destitution will create comparing structures as far as you could tell, except if you hold to the reality that there is no neediness; there is just overflow. To think of well-being when encircled by the appearances of illness, or to think of wealth when amidst appearances of neediness, requires influence; however, he who secures this influence turns into a Driving force. An idea, in this substance, delivers what is imaged by the idea. Man can frame things in his idea, and, by presenting his thinking for undefined substance, can cause what he thinks is going to be made. It might very well be inquired as to whether I can demonstrate these assertions; and without delving into subtleties, I answer that I can do as such, both by rationale and experience. Thinking back from the peculiarities of structure and thought, I come to one unique reasoning substance; and thinking forward from this thinking substance, I come to labor supply to cause the arrangement of what he thinks about. What's more, by exploring, I view the thinking as valid; and this is my most grounded confirmation. Assuming the person who peruses this book gets rich by doing everything that it tells him to do, that is proof on the side of my case; yet assuming each man who does everything that it tells him to do gets rich, that is positive verification until somebody goes through the cycle and comes up short.

The hypothesis is valid until the interaction comes up short; and this cycle won't fall flat, for each man who does precisely the exact thing this book advises him to do will get rich. I have said that men get rich by getting things done with a particular goal in mind; and to do as such, men should become ready to think with a specific goal in mind. A man's approach to doing things is the immediate consequence of the manner in which he contemplates things. To get things done in a manner you maintain that should do them, you should procure the capacity to think in the manner in which you need to think; this is the most important move toward getting rich. To think what you need to believe is to think TRUTH, paying little heed to appearances. Each man has the normal and intrinsic ability to think what he needs to think, however, he expects definitely more work to do as such than it

does to think about the contemplations which are proposed by appearances. To think as indicated by appearance is simple; to think truth paying little mind to appearances is relentless and requires the consumption of more power than some other work man is called upon to perform. There is no work from which a great many people shrivel as they do from that of supported and sequential ideas; it is the hardest work on the planet. This is particularly evident when the truth is in opposition to appearances. Each appearance in the noticeable world will in general create a comparing structure in the psyche that notices it; this must be forestalled by holding the possibility of Reality. To view the presence of sickness will create the type of illness as far as you could tell, and at last in your body, except if you hold the prospect of reality, which is that there is no sickness; it is just an appearance, and actually wellbeing. To view the appearances of destitution will deliver related structures as far as you could tell, except if you hold to the reality that there is no neediness; there is just overflow. To think of well-being when encircled by the appearances of sickness, or to think of wealth when amidst appearances of destitution, requires influence; however, he who gets this influence turns into a Brains.

He can overcome destiny; he can have anything he desires. This power must be procured by getting hold of the essential truth which is behind all appearances; and that reality is that there is one Reasoning Substance, from which and by which everything is made. Then we should understand the reality that each thought held in this substance turns into a structure, and that man can so present his contemplations for it as to make them take structure and become noticeable things. At the point when we understand this, we lose all uncertainty and dread, for we realize that we can make what we need to make; we can get what we need to have and can become what we need to be. As an initial move toward getting rich, you should trust the three central

articulations are given already in this section, and to stress them. I rehash them here: There is reasoning stuff from which everything is made, and which, in its unique state, pervades, enters, and fills the interspaces of the universe. An idea, in this substance, delivers what is imaged by the idea. Man can shape things in his idea, and, by putting forth his thinking for undefined substance, can cause what he thinks is going to be made. You should dismiss any remaining ideas of the universe other than this monistic one, and you should stay upon this until it is fixed to you and has turned into your routine thought. Peruse these belief proclamations over once more; fix each word upon your memory, and think upon them until you solidly accept what they say. On the off chance that uncertainty comes to you, cast it to the side as a transgression.

Try not to pay attention to contentions against this thought; don't go to chapels or talks where an opposite idea of things is instructed or taught. Try not to understand magazines or books which show an alternate thought; on the off chance that you get stirred up in your confidence, every one of your endeavors will be to no end. Try not to inquire as to why these things are valid, nor conjecture regarding how they can be valid; essentially accept them based on previous experience. The study of getting rich starts with the outright acknowledgment of this confidence.

Chapter 5

Expanding Life.

. YOU should dispose of the last remnant of the old thought that there is a Divinity whose will it is that you ought to be poor, or whose reasons might be served by keeping you in destitution. The Canny Substance which is All, and on the whole, and which day-to-day routines on the whole and lives in you, is a deliberately Living Substance. Being an intentionally living substance, It should have the nature and inborn craving of every living insight for the increment of life. Each living thing must ceaselessly look for the development of its life, since life, in the simple demonstration of living, should build itself. A seed dropped into the ground, springs into movement, and in the demonstration of living produces 100 additional seeds; life, by living, duplicates itself. It is always Turning out to be More; it should do as such, on the off chance that it keeps on being by any stretch of the imagination. Insight is under this equivalent need for persistent increment. Each thought we figure makes it essential for us to think one more thought; awareness is persistently growing. Each reality we learn drives us to the learning of another reality; information is constantly expanding. Each ability we develop brings to the brain the longing to develop another ability; we are dependent upon the inclination of life, looking for articulation, which at any point drives us on to know more, to accomplish more, and to be more. To know more, accomplish more, and be more we should have more; we should have things to use, for we learn, do, and become, exclusively by utilizing things. We should get rich, with the goal to live more. The craving for wealth is just the limit with respect to bigger life looking for satisfaction; each wants is the work of an unexpressed chance to come right into it. It is power trying to show which causes want. That which gets you to need more cash flow is equivalent to that which makes the plant develop; it is Life, looking for more full articulation.

The One Living Substance should be dependent upon this intrinsic law of all life; it is pervaded with the longing to live more; to that end, it is under the need of making things. The One Substance wants to live more in you; subsequently, it believes that you should have everything you can utilize. It is the longing of God that you ought to get rich. He believes that you should get rich since he can communicate his thoughts better through you assuming you have a lot of things to use in giving him articulation. He can live more in you assuming you have limitless order of the method for life. The universe wants you to have all that you need to have. Nature is well disposed to your arrangements. Everything is normal for you. Decide that this is valid. It is fundamental, but your motivation ought to blend with the reason that is inAll You should need reality, not the simple delight of arousing satisfaction. Life is the presentation of capability; and the individual truly lives just when he carries out each role, physical, mental, and otherworldly, of which he is able, without overabundance in any. You would rather not set rich up to live boorishly, for the satisfaction of creature wants; that isn't life. Yet, the presentation of each and every actual capability is a piece of life, and nobody lives totally who prevents the motivations from getting the body an ordinary and invigorating articulation. You would rather not get rich exclusively to appreciate mental joys, to get information, to delight desire, to surpass others, to be well known. Every one of these is a real piece of life, however, the one who lives for the joys of the mind alone will just have a half-life, and he won't ever be happy with his parcel.

You would rather not get rich exclusively to ultimately benefit others, to lose yourself for the salvation of humankind, to encounter the delights of altruism and penance. The delights of the spirit are just a piece of life, and they are no greater or nobler than some other part. You need to get wealthy all together that you might eat, drink, and be cheerful when the time has come to do these things; all together that you might encircle yourself with delightful things, see far-off lands, feed your psyche, and foster your keenness; all together that you might cherish men and do kind things, and have the option to have a decent impact in assisting the world with tracking down the truth. In any case, recollect that outrageous philanthropy is no greater and no nobler than outrageous narrow-mindedness; both are botches. Dispose of God's desired thought to forfeit yourself for other people, and you can get his approval thus; God doesn't require anything of the sort. What he needs is that you ought to capitalize on yourself, as far as yourself might be concerned, and for other people; and you can help other people more by taking full advantage of yourself than in different ways. You can capitalize on yourself exclusively by getting rich; so it is correct and admirable that you ought to give your first and best thought crafted by obtaining abundance. Keep in mind, notwithstanding, that the longing of Substance is for all, and its developments should be for more life to all; it can't be made to work for less life to any, on the grounds that it is similarly altogether, looking for wealth and life. Canny Substance will make things for you, however, it won't remove things from another person and give them to you. You should dispose of the prospect of rivalry. You are to make, not to seek what is as of now made. You don't need to remove anything from anyone. You don't need to drive sharp deals.

You don't need to cheat, or make use of it. You don't have to allow any man to work for you for short of what he procures. You don't need to desire the property of others, or to take a gander at it with impractical eyes; no man has anything of which you can't have the like, and that without removing what he has from him. You are to turn into a maker, not a contender; you will get what you need, yet so that when you get it each and every other man will have more than he has now. I'm mindful that there are men who get an immense measure of cash by continuing contrary to the assertions in the section above and may add an expression of clarification here. Men of the plutocratic kind, who become exceptionally rich, do so at times absolutely by their remarkable capacity on the plane of the contest; and in some cases, they unknowingly relate themselves to Substance in its extraordinary purposes and developments for the overall racial upbuilding through modern advancement. Rockefeller, Carnegie, Morgan, et al., have been the oblivious specialists of the Preeminent in the essential work of arranging and coordinating useful industry; and eventually, their work will contribute enormously toward expanded life for all.

Their day is almost finished; they have coordinated creation, and will before long be prevailed by the specialists of the huge number, who will sort out the apparatus of appropriation. The multi-moguls resemble the beast reptiles of ancient times; they have a fundamental impact in the transformative cycle, yet a similar Power that delivered them will discard them. What's more, it is well to remember that they have never been truly rich; a record of the confidential existences of the vast majority of this class will show that they have truly been the most miserable and pitiable of poor people. Wealth got on the cutthroat plane is rarely palatable and super durable; they are yours today, and another's tomorrow. Keep in mind, in the event that you are to become wealthy in a logical and certain manner, you should rise completely out of the cutthroat idea. You should never think briefly that the stockpile is restricted. Right when you start to feel that all the cash is being "cornered" and constrained by financiers and others and that you

should endeavor to get regulations passed to stop this cycle, etc; at that time you drop into the serious brain, and your ability to cause creation is away until further notice; and what is more terrible, you will most likely capture the innovative developments you have proactively initiatedRealize that there is the endless huge number of dollars of gold in the mountains of the earth, not yet exposed; and know that in the event that there were not, more would be made from Figuring Substance to supply your requirements. Realize that the cash you really want will come, regardless of whether it is vital for 1,000 men to be directed to the revelation of new mother lodes tomorrow. Never take a gander at the noticeable stock; take a gander at the boundless wealth in Undefined Substance, and Realize that they are coming to you as quickly as you can get and utilize them.No one, by cornering the apparent inventory, can keep you from getting what is yours. So never permit yourself to think for a moment that the very best structure spots will be taken before you prepare to fabricate your home, except if you rush. Never stress over the trusts and consolidates, and get restless for dread they will before long come to claim the entire earth. Never get apprehensive that you will lose what you need since another individual "outsmarts you". That couldn't really occur; you are not looking for whatever is moved by any other person; you are causing what you need to be made from an Undefined Substance, and the stockpile is unbounded. Adhere to the figured-out assertion:- - There is reasoning stuff from which everything is made, and which, in its unique state, saturates, enters, and fills the interspaces of the universe. An idea, in this substance, delivers what is imaged by the idea. Man can frame things in his idea, and, by presenting his thinking for amorphous substance, can cause what he thinks is going to be made.

Chapter .6

How Wealth Comes to You.

At the point when I say that you don't need to drive sharp deals, I don't imply that you need to drive no deals by any means, or that you are over the need for having any dealings with your kindred men. I imply that you won't have to manage them unjustifiably; you don't need to get something for little more than, can provide for each man more than you take from him. You can't give each man more in real money market esteem than you take from him, yet you can give him more being used worth than the money worth of what you take from him. The paper, ink, and other material in this book may not merit the cash you pay for it; yet on the off chance that the thoughts recommended by it bring you a large number of dollars, you have not been violated by the people who offered it to you; they have given you an extraordinary use an incentive for a little money esteem. Allow us to assume that I own an image by one of the extraordinary craftsmen, which, in any edified local area, is worth a great many dollars. I take it to Baffin Beam, and by "charismatic skill" prompt an Eskimo to give a heap of furs worth $500 for it. I have truly violated him, for he has no need for the image; it has no utilization worth to him; it won't add to his life. However, assume I give him a weapon worth $50 for his furs; then he has made a decent deal. He has a need for the firearm; it will get him a lot more furs and much food; it will add to his life inside and out; it will make him rich. At the point when you ascend from the serious to the imaginative plane, you can filter your deals rigorously, and assuming you are selling any man anything which doesn't add more to his life than what he gives you in return, you can stand to stop it. You don't need to beat anyone in business. What's more, in the event that you are in a business that beats individuals, receive in return without a moment's delay.

Give each man more being used worth than you take from him in real money esteem; then you are adding to the existence of the world by each deal. . Assuming you have individuals working for you, you should take from them more in real money esteem than you pay them in compensation; yet you can so coordinate your business that it will be loaded up with the standard of progression, thus that every representative who wishes to do so may propel a little consistently. You can cause your business to accomplish for your workers how this book is doing you. You can lead your business as a kind of stepping stool, by which each worker who will take the difficulty might move to wealth himself; and offered the chance, in the event that he won't do as such, it isn't your issue. Lastly, in light of the fact that you are to cause the production of your wealth from an Undefined Substance that pervades all your current circumstances, it doesn't follow that they are to come to fruition from the environment and appear before your eyes. In the event that you need a sewing machine, for example, I don't intend to let you know that you are to dazzle the possibility of a sewing machine on Thinking Substance until the machine is framed without hands, in the room where you sit, or somewhere else. In any case, assuming that you need a sewing machine, hold the psychological picture of it with the best conviction that it is being made, or is headed to you. After once shaping the idea, have the most outright and unquestioning confidence that the sewing machine is coming; never think about it, or talk of it, in some other way than as being certain to show up.

Guarantee it as currently yours. It will be brought to you by the force of the Incomparable Insight, following up on the personalities of men. Assuming you live in Maine, it is possible that a man will be brought from Texas or Japan to participate in some exchange which will bring about your getting what you need. Provided that this is true, the entire matter will be as a lot to that man's benefit for all intents and purposes to yours. Remember briefly that the Reasoning

Substance is through all, on the whole, speaking with all, and can impact all. The craving for Reasoning Substance for a more full life and better living has caused the making of all the sewing machines previously made; it can cause the production of millions more,

What's more, at whatever point men put it into high gear by want and confidence, and by acting with a particular goal in mind. You can positively have a sewing machine in your home, and it is similarly as sure that you can have some other thing or things which you need, and which you will use for the headway of your own life and the existence of others. You really want not to hold back about asking generally; "It is your Dad's pleasure to give you the realm, " said Jesus. Unique Substance needs to experience all that is conceivable in you, and believes you should have everything you can or will use for living the most plentiful life. Assuming you fix upon your awareness the way that the longing you feel for the ownership of wealth is unified with the craving of Supremacy for more complete articulation, your confidence becomes invulnerable.

When I saw a young man sitting at a piano, and pointlessly attempting to deliver congruence once again from the keys; I saw that he was lamenting and incited by his failure to play genuine music. I asked him the reason for his vexation, and he replied, "I can feel the music in me, yet I can't make my hands go right." The music in him was the Desire for Unique Substance, containing every one of the potential outcomes of all life; all that there is of music was looking for articulation through the youngster. God, the One Substance, is attempting to live and do and appreciate things through mankind. He is saying "I believe that hands should fabricate superb designs, to play divine harmonies, to arrange radiant pictures; I believe that feet should get my things done, eyes to see my delights, tongues to tell powerful bits of insight and to sing great melodies, etc. All that there is of plausibility is looking for articulation through men. God needs the people who can play music to have pianos and each and every other instrument, and to possess the ability to develop their gifts to the furthest reaches; He needs the individuals who can see the value in excellence to have the option to encircle themselves with wonderful things; He needs the people who can perceive truth to have each an amazing open door to travel and notice; He needs the individuals who can see the value in dress

to be perfectly dressed, and the people who can see the value in great food to be lavishly taken care of. He needs everything since Himself appreciates and values them; God needs to play, sing, and appreciate magnificence, declare truth and wear fine garments, and eat great food sources. "It is God that worketh in you to will and to do," said Paul. The craving you feel for wealth is endless, looking to communicate his thoughts in you as He tried to track down articulation in the young man at the piano. So you want not to hold back to a great extent. Your part is to center and communicate the craving to

God. This is a troublesome point with the vast majority; they hold something of the old thought that neediness and selflessness are satisfying to God. They view destitution as a piece of the arrangement, a need of nature. They have the possibility that God has completed His work, and made everything that could be made, and that most men should remain poor since it isn't sufficient to go around. They hold to such a great deal of this wrong feeling that they feel embarrassed to request riches; they do whatever it takes not to need in excess of an exceptionally humble skill, barely enough to make them genuinely agreeable. I review now the instance of one understudy who was informed that he should get as a main priority an unmistakable image of the things he wanted, so the imaginative idea of them may be dazzled on Nebulous Substance. He was an exceptionally unfortunate man, residing in a leased house, and having just what he procured from one day to another; and he was unable to embrace the way that all abundance was his. Thus, subsequent to thoroughly considering the matter, he concluded that he could sensibly request another carpet for the floor of his best room, and an anthracite coal oven to warm the house during the chilly climate. Adhering to the directions given in this book, he got these things in a couple of months; and afterward, it unfolded upon him that he had not asked enough. He went through the house in which he resided, and arranged every one of the upgrades he might want to make in it; he intellectually added a narrows window here and a room there, until it

was finished to him as his optimal home; and afterward, he arranged its decorations. Holding the entire picture to himself, he started residing in the Specific Way, and pushing toward what he needed; and possesses the house now, and is remaking it after the type of his psychological picture. What's more, presently, with still bigger confidence, he is proceeding to get more prominent things. It has been unto him as per his confidence, and it is so with you and with us all.

Chapter.7

Appreciation.

THE outlines given in the last part will have passed on to the peruser the way that the most important move toward finding out about your needs to the Undefined Substance. This is valid, and you will see that to do so it becomes important to relate yourself to the Nebulous Knowledge in an amicable manner. Getting this agreeable connection involves such essential and crucial significance that I will give space to its conversation here, and give you guidelines which, assuming that you will follow them, will be sure to bring you into ideal solidarity of the psyche with God. The entire course of mental change and penance can be summarized in a single word, appreciation. To begin with, you accept that there is one Keen Substance, from which all things continue; second, you accept that this Substance gives you all that you want; and third, you relate yourself to it by a sensation of profound and significant appreciation. Many individuals who request their lives properly in any remaining ways are kept in destitution by their absence of appreciation. Having gotten one gift from God, they cut the wires which interface them with Him by neglecting to make an affirmation. It is straightforward that the closer we live to the wellspring of abundance, the more abundance we will get; and it is simple additionally to comprehend that the spirit that is generally appreciative lives in nearer contact with God than the one which never focuses on Him in grateful affirmation. The more appreciatively we fix our brains on the Incomparable when beneficial things come to us, the more beneficial things we will get, and the more quickly they will come; the explanation basically is that the psychological mentality of appreciation brings the brain into nearer contact with the source from which the gifts come.

Assuming it is a groundbreaking insight to you that appreciation brings your entire brain into nearer congruence with the inventive energies of the universe, think of it as well, and you will see that it is valid. The beneficial things you as of now have come to you along the line of acquiescence to specific regulations. Appreciation will lead your psyche out along the ways by which things come, and it will keep you as one with innovative ideas and keep you from falling into serious ideas. Appreciation alone can keep you looking toward the All, and keep you from falling into the mistake of reasoning the stock as restricted, and to do that would be deadly to your expectations. There is a Law of Appreciation, and it is totally important that you ought to notice the law, assuming that you are to come by the outcomes you look for. The law of appreciation is the regular rule that activity and response are generally equivalent and in inverse bearings. The thankful exceeding of your psyche in grateful commendation to the Preeminent is freedom or use of power; it can't neglect to arrive at that to which it tended to, and the response is a momentary development towards you. "Draw near unto God, and He will draw near unto you." That is an assertion of mental truth. Furthermore, in the event that your appreciation is solid and steady, the response in Nebulous Substance will be areas of strength to be persistent; the development of the things you need will be generally toward you. Notice the appreciative demeanor that Jesus took; how He generally is by all accounts saying "I say thanks to You, Father, that Thou hearest me." You can't practice a lot of force without appreciation; for appreciation keeps you associated with Power. However, the worth of appreciation doesn't comprise exclusively in getting you more gifts from now on. Without appreciation, you can't long keep from disappointed thoughts seeing things as they are. The second you license your psyche to stay disappointed in things as they are, you start to lose ground. You fix

consideration upon the normal, the standard, poor people, and the abhorrent and mean; and your brain appears as these things. Then, at that point, you will communicate these structures or mental pictures to the Shapeless, and the normal, poor people, the foul, and mean will come to you. To allow your psyche to stay at the second rate is to become mediocre and to encircle yourself with sub-par things. Then again, to fix your consideration of the best is to encircle yourself with the best, and to turn into the best. The Inventive Power inside us makes us into the picture of that to which we offer our consideration. We are Thinking Substance, and thinking substance generally appears as that which it ponders. The thankful brain is continually fixed upon the best; consequently, it will in general turn into the best; it takes the structure or character of the best, and will get the best.

Additionally, confidence is brought into the world of appreciation. The thankful psyche constantly anticipates beneficial things, and the assumption becomes confidence. The response of appreciation upon one's own psyche produces confidence; and each friendly influx of appreciative thanksgiving increments confidence. He who has no sensation of appreciation can't long hold a living confidence; and without a living confidence, you can't get rich by the imaginative technique, as we will find in the accompanying sections. It is important, then, to develop the propensity for being appreciative of each beneficial thing that comes to you, and to ceaselessly offer gratitude. What's more, since all things have added to your progression, you ought to remember everything for your appreciation. Try not to sit around idly thinking or discussing the weaknesses or wrong activities of tycoons or trust magnates. Their association with the world has created your open door; all you get truly comes to you as a result of them.

Try not to seethe against degenerate legislators; on the off chance that it was not for lawmakers we ought to fall into an insurgency, and your chance would be extraordinarily diminished. God has worked quite a while and persistently to bring us up to where we are in industry and government, and He is going right on with His work. There isn't the least uncertainty that He will get rid of tycoons, trust magnates, chiefs of industry, and legislators when they can be saved; yet meanwhile, view - they are generally excellent. Recollect that they are assisting with orchestrating the lines of transmission along which your wealth will come to you, and be appreciative of them all. This will carry you into agreeable relations with the positive qualities in all things, and the positive qualities in all that will advance toward you.

Chapter .8

Thinking in a Specific Manner.

TURN around to section six and read again the narrative of the one who framed a psychological picture of his home, and you will find out about the underlying move toward getting rich. You should shape an unmistakable and positive mental image of what you need; you can't send a thought except if you have it yourself. You should have it before you can give it; and many individuals disappoint Thinking Substance since they have just an obscure and foggy idea of the things they need to do, to have, or to turn into. It isn't enough that you ought to want abundance "to accomplish something beneficial with"; everyone has that longing. It isn't enough that you ought to have the wish to travel, see things, live more, and so forth.

Everyone has those wants too. On the off chance that you planned to send a remote message to a companion, you wouldn't send the letters of the letter set in their request, and let him build the directive for himself; nor would you take words indiscriminately from the word reference. You would send a reasonable sentence; one which implied something. At the point when you attempt to put forth your needs for Substance, recall that it should be finished by an intelligible proclamation; you should understand what you need, and be clear. You can never get rich, or begin the imaginative influence right into it, by conveying unformed longings and unclear cravings.

Go over your longings similarly as the man I have portrayed went over his home; see exactly what you need, and get an unmistakable mental image of it as you wish it to look when you get it. That unmistakable mental picture you should have consistently as a top priority, as the mariner has as a primary concern the port toward which he is cruising the boat; you should keep your face toward it constantly. You should no more fail to focus on it than the pilot fails to focus on the compass. It isn't important to take practice in that frame of mind, to separate extraordinary times for supplication and certification, nor to "go into

the quiet," nor to do mysterious tricks of any sort. These things are all around ok, yet all you want is to understand what you need and to need it gravely enough with the goal that it will remain in your viewpoint. Spend however much of your relaxation time that you can be considering your image, yet nobody needs to take activities to focus his brain on a thing which he truly needs; it is the things you couldn't care less about which expect work to fix your consideration upon them. What's more, except if you truly need to get rich, with the goal that the craving is sufficiently able to hold your considerations coordinated to the reason as the attractive post holds the needle of the compass, it will scarcely be worthwhile for you to attempt to do the guidelines given in this book. The techniques in this put forward are for individuals whose craving for wealth is sufficiently able to beat mental apathy and the affection for straightforwardness and make them work. The more clear and unmistakable you make your image then, and the more you stay upon it, drawing out the entirety of its superb subtleties, the more grounded your longing will be; and the more grounded your craving, the simpler it will be to hold your brain fixed upon the image of what you need. Something more is essential, in any case, than just seeing the image. If that is all you do, you are just a visionary and will have practically zero power for achievement. Behind your unmistakable vision should be the reason to acknowledge it; to bring it out in substantial articulation. Also, behind this reason should be an invulnerable and relentless Confidence that the thing is as of now yours; that it is "within reach" and you have just to claim it. Live in the new house, intellectually, until it takes structure around you truly. In the psychological domain, enter the double into full satisfaction in the things you need. "At all things, ye request when ye ask, accept that ye get them, and ye will have them," said Jesus.

See the things you need as though they were entirely you constantly; view yourself as purchasing and utilizing them. Utilize them in a creative mind similarly as you will utilize them when they are your unmistakable belongings. Abide upon your psychological picture until it is clear and unmistakable, and afterward take the Psychological Demeanor of Proprietorship toward everything in that image. Claim it, at the top of the priority list, in full confidence that it is really yours. Hold to this psychological proprietorship; don't waiver for a moment in the confidence that it is genuine. Furthermore, recall information disclosed in a procedure part about appreciation; be as grateful for it all the time as you hope to be the point at which it has taken structure. The one who can earnestly say thanks to God for the things which at this point he claims just in creative mind, has genuine confidence. He will get rich; he will cause the production of all he needs. You don't have to implore more than once for things you need; informing God consistently isn't required. "Utilize not vain redundancies as the rapscallion do," said Jesus shared with his understudies, "for your Dad knoweth that ye have need of these things before ye ask Him." Your part is to wisely form your longing for the things which make for a bigger life, and to get these cravings organized into a cognizant entire; and afterward to present this Entire Longing for the Undefined Substance, which has the power and the will to bring you what you need. You don't establish this connection by rehashing a series of words; you make it by holding the vision with unflinching Reason to accomplish it, and with ardent Confidence that you in all actuality do achieve it. The solution to petitioning heaven isn't as per your confidence while you are talking, yet as indicated by your confidence while you are working. You can't dazzle the brain of God by having a unique day off put aside to let him know what you need, and afterward failing to remember Him during the remainder of the week. You can't dazzle Him by having extraordinary hours to go into your storage room and implore, if

you then, at that point, excuse the matter from your brain until the hour of petitioning heaven returns once more. Oral petitioning heaven is alright, and makes its difference, particularly upon yourself, in explaining your vision and fortifying your confidence; yet it isn't your oral petitions which get you what you need. To get rich you needn't bother with a "sweet hour of supplication"; you really want to "ask consistently." And by petition, I mean holding consistently to your vision, with the reason to cause its creation into a strong structure, and the confidence that you are doing as such. "Accept that ye get them." The entire matter turns on when you have plainly shaped your vision. At the point when you have shaped it, it is best to offer an oral expression, tending to the Preeminent in the respectful petition; and from that second you should, as a main priority, get what you request. Live in the new house; wear fine garments; ride in the car; go on the excursion, and unhesitatingly plan for more noteworthy excursions. Think and discuss everything you have requested regarding genuine present possession. Envision a climate, and a monetary condition precisely as you need them, and experience constantly in that nonexistent climate and monetary condition. Mind, nonetheless, that you don't do this as a simple visionary and visionary; hold to the Confidence that the nonexistent is being understood, and to the Reason to acknowledge it. Recollect that it is confidence and reason in the utilization of the creative mind which has the effect between the researcher and the visionary. Furthermore, having realized this reality, it is here that you should get familiar with the appropriate utilization of the Will.

Chapter .9

Step-by-step instructions to Utilize the Will.

To begin getting wealthy in a logical manner, you don't attempt to apply your resolve to anything beyond yourself. In any case, you reserve no privilege to do as such. It is inappropriate to apply your will to different people, to inspire them to do what you wish done. It is as blatantly off-base to constrain individuals by mental power for all intents and purposes to pressure them by actual power. On the off chance that convincing individuals by actual power to get things done for you decreases them to subjection, convincing them by mental means achieves the very same thing; the main distinction is in strategies. Assuming that taking things from individuals by actual power is theft, then taking things by mental power is burglary additionally; there is no distinction on a basic level.

You reserve no option to utilize your resolve upon someone else, even "to his benefit"; for you don't have the foggiest idea what is for his benefit. The study of getting rich doesn't expect you to apply influence or power to some other individual, in any capacity at all. There isn't the smallest need for doing as such; without a doubt, any endeavor to utilize your will upon others will simply will more often than not route your motivation. You don't have to apply your will to things, to urge them to come to you. That would just be attempting to force God and would be stupid and pointless, as well as flippant. You don't need to propel God to give you beneficial things, anything other than you need to utilize your determination to make the sunrise. You don't need to utilize your resolution to overcome a threatening divinity or to cause difficult and insubordinate powers to do your offering.

The substance is well disposed to you and is more restless to give you what you need than you are to get it. To get rich, you really just want to utilize your self-discipline. At the point when you know what to think and do, then, at that point, you should utilize your will to urge yourself to think and do the right things. That is the authentic utilization of the will in getting what you need - - to involve it in holding yourself to the right course. Utilize your will to keep yourself thinking and acting in the Specific Manner. Try not to attempt to project your will, your contemplations, or your brain out into space, to "act" on things or individuals.

Keep your psyche at home; it can achieve more there than somewhere else. Utilize your psyche to frame a psychological picture of what you need, hold that vision with confidence and reason; and utilize your will to keep your brain working in the Correct Manner. The more consistent and nonstop your confidence and reason, the more quickly you will get rich since you will establish just Certain connections upon

Substance, and you won't kill or counterbalance them with bad introductions.

The image of your longings, held with confidence and design, is taken up by the Amorphous and pervades it to huge spans - all through the universe, as far as I might be aware. As this impression spreads, everything is set pushing toward its acknowledgment; each living thing, each lifeless thing, and the things yet uncreated are mixed toward creating what you need. All power starts to be applied like that; everything starts to push toward you. The personalities of individuals, all over the place, are impacted toward doing the things important to the satisfying of your longings; and they work for you, unwittingly. However, you can really take a look at this by beginning a bad introduction to the Nebulous Substance. Uncertainty or unbelief is as sure to begin a development away from you as confidence and design are to begin one toward you. By not understanding this a great many people who attempt to utilize "mental science" to get rich make them disappointed. Consistently and second you spend in giving regard to questions and fears, consistently you spend in stress, consistently in which your spirit is moved by unbelief, sets a current away from you in the entire space of shrewd Substance. Every one of the commitments is unto them that accept, and unto them, as it were. Notice how unyielding Jesus was upon this place of conviction, and presently you know the motivation behind why. Since conviction is immensely significant, common sense would suggest that you should monitor your considerations; and as your convictions will be formed to an exceptionally incredible degree by the things you notice and contemplate, you just ought to order your consideration. Furthermore, here the will comes into utilization; for it is by your will that you decide upon what things your consideration will be fixed. If you have any desire to become rich, you should not investigate destitution. Things are not created by contemplating their alternate extremes. Well-being is never to be achieved by concentrating on infection and contemplating illness; honesty isn't to be advanced by concentrating on wrongdoing and pondering sin; and nobody at any point got rich by concentrating on neediness and contemplating destitution. Medication as a study of infection has expanded illness; religion as a study of wrongdoing has advanced sin, and financial matters as an investigation of neediness will fill the world with horror and need. Try not to discuss neediness; don't research it, or fret about it. Quit worrying about what its causes are; you don't have anything to do with them. What concerns you is the fix. Try not to invest your energy in altruistic work, or good cause developments; all foundations just will in general propagate the horror it means to destroy. I don't say that you ought to be unfeeling or harsh, and decline to hear the call of need; however, you should make an effort not to kill

destitution in any of the regular ways. Put neediness behind you, and put all that relates to it behind you, and "make great." Get rich; that is the most effective way you can help poor people. What's more, you can't hold the psychological picture which is to make you rich assuming you fill your brain with pictures of neediness. Try not to understand books or papers which give incidental records of the awfulness of the apartment inhabitants, of the abhorrence of kid work, etc. Guess what nothing fills you might think with bleak pictures of need and languishing. You can't help the poor in that frame of mind by being familiar with these things, and the far and wide information on them doesn't tend by any means to get rid of neediness. What will in general get rid of neediness isn't the getting of pictures of destitution into your psyche, yet getting pictures of abundance into the personalities of poor people. You are not abandoning the poor in their hopelessness when you will not permit your psyche to be loaded up with photos of that wretchedness. Destitution should be possible with, not by expanding the number of wealthy individuals who contemplate neediness, yet by expanding the number of destitute individuals who reason with confidence to get rich. The poor don't require a noble cause; they need motivation.

Noble cause just sends them a portion of bread to keep them alive in their horror, or gives them a diversion to cause them to forget for a little while; however, motivation will make them emerge from their wretchedness. If you have any desire to help poor people, show them that they can become rich; demonstrate it by getting rich yourself. The main manner by which neediness will at any point be expelled from this world is by getting an enormous and continually expanding number of individuals to rehearse the lessons of this book. Individuals should be educated to become rich by creation, not by rivalry. Each man who becomes rich by contest tosses down behind him the stepping stool by which he rises, and holds others down; however, every man who gets rich by creation opens a way for thousands to follow him and motivates them to do as such. You are not showing cruelty or a barbarous demeanor when you won't feel sorry for destitution, see neediness, read about neediness, think or discuss it, or pay attention to the people who in all actuality do discuss it. Utilize your self-control to keep your brain Beside the point of destitution, and to keep it fixed with confidence and reason ON the vision of what you need.

Chapter. 10

Further Utilization of the Will.

YOU can't hold a valid and clear vision of riches in the event that you are continually directing your concentration toward restricting pictures, whether they be outside or nonexistent. Try not to recount your previous difficulties of a monetary sort, on the off chance that you have had them. Try not to think about them by any means. Try not to recount the neediness of your folks or the difficulties of your initial life; to do any of these things is to intellectually class yourself with the poor for the present, and it will unquestionably look at the development of things toward you. "Allow the dead to cover their dead," Jesus said. Put destitution and everything that relates to neediness totally behind you. You have acknowledged a specific hypothesis of the universe as being right, and are resting every one of your expectations of satisfaction on its being right; and what might you at any point acquire by giving notice to clashing speculations? Try not to peruse strict books which let you know that the world is before long reaching a conclusion, and don't peruse the composition of mud slingers and cynical logicians who let you know that it is going to Satan. The world won't be Satan; it is going to God. It is brilliant Becoming. Valid, there might be decent numerous things in existing circumstances which are unpleasant; yet what is the utilization of concentrating on them when they are unquestionably dying, and when the investigation of them just will in general really look at their passing and keep them with us? Why concentrate entirely on things which are being eliminated by transformative development, when you can't hurry their evacuation exclusively by advancing the developmental development to the extent that your piece of it goes?

Regardless of how horrendous it might be to circumstances in specific nations, segments, or places, you burn through your time and annihilate your own possibilities by thinking about them. You ought to show yourself the world's becoming rich. Consider the wealth the world is coming into, rather than the destitution it is outgrowing; and remember that the main manner by which you can help the world in developing rich is by developing rich yourself through the imaginative strategy - - not the cutthroat one. Offer your consideration entirely to wealth; overlook neediness. At the point when you think or discuss the people who are poor, think and talk about them as the individuals who are becoming rich; as the people who are to be praised instead of felt sorry for. Then, at that point, they and others will get the motivation, and start to look for an exit plan. Since I say that you are to give your entire time and brain and thought to wealth, it doesn't follow that you are to be shameful or mean. To turn out to be truly rich is the noblest point you can have throughout everyday life, for it incorporates all the other things. On the serious plane, the battle to get rich is a Heathen scramble for control over different men; yet when we come into the innovative brain, this is changed. All that is conceivable in the method of significance and soul unfoldment, of administration and grandiose undertaking, stops via getting rich; everything is made conceivable by the utilization of things. Assuming you need it for actual well-being, you will observe that the achievement of it is contingent on your getting rich. Just the people who are liberated from monetary concern, and who possess the ability to carry on with a lighthearted presence and follow sterile practices, can have and hold well-being.

Moral and otherworldly significance is conceivable just to the individuals who are over the cutthroat fight for presence, and just the people who are becoming rich on the plane of inventive ideas are liberated from the debasing impacts of the contest. On the off chance that your heart is set on homegrown bliss, recall that affection thrives best where there is refinement, an elevated degree of thought, and independence from ruining impacts; and these are to be found just where wealth is achieved by the activity of innovative ideas, without hardship or competition. You can't target anything so extraordinary or respectable, I rehash, as to become rich; and you should fix your consideration upon your psychological image of wealth, to the avoidance of all that might generally diminish or darken the vision. You should figure out how to see the hidden TRUTH no matter what; you should see underneath all apparently off-base circumstances, the Incomparable One Life truly pushing ahead toward more full articulation and more complete satisfaction. It is the reality that there is no such thing as neediness; that there is just abundance. Certain individuals stay in destitution since they are oblivious to the way that there is abundance for them, and these can best be educated by showing them the way to prosperity in their own individual and practice. Others are poor in light of the fact that, while they feel that there is an exit plan, they are excessively mentally sluggish to invest the psychological energy important to track down like that and travel by it; and for these everything things you can manage is to stir their longing by showing them the satisfaction that comes from being properly rich. Others actually are poor in light of the fact that, while they have some thought of science, they have become so overwhelmed and lost in the labyrinth of magical and mysterious speculations that they don't know which street to take. They attempt a combination of numerous frameworks and flop on the whole. For these, once more, the absolute best thing to do is to show the correct way in your own individual and practice; an ounce of doing things merits a pound of conjecturing.

The absolute smartest option for the entire world is to capitalize on yourself. You can serve God and man in not any more compelling manner than by getting rich; that is, assuming you get rich by the imaginative strategy and not by the cutthroat one. Something else. We affirm that this book gives exhaustively the standards of the study of getting rich; and assuming that is valid, you don't have to peruse some other book on the subject. This might sound thin and narcissistic, yet consider: there is not any more logical strategy for calculation in math than by expansion, deduction, augmentation, and division; no other technique is conceivable. There can nevertheless be one briefest distance between two focuses. There is just a single method for thinking deductively, and that is to think in the way that leads by the most immediate and straightforward course to the objective. No man has yet figured out a briefer or less mind-boggling "framework" than the one put forward in this; it has been deprived of all trivial items. At the point when you begin on this, lay regardless of others; reset your head by and large. Peruse this book consistently; keep it with you; commit it to memory, and don't contemplate other "frameworks" and speculations. Assuming that you do, you will start to feel a little wary, and to be questionable and faltering in your idea; and afterward, you will start to make disappointments. After you have made great and become rich, you might concentrate on different frameworks however much you please; yet until you are very certain that you have acquired what you need, read nothing on this line except for this book, except if it is the writers referenced in the Prelude. Also, read just the most hopeful remarks on the world's news; those together as one with your image. Likewise, delay your examinations concerning the mysterious. Try not to fiddle with theosophy, Mysticism, or fellow studies. Almost certainly, the dead actually live, and are close; yet assuming that they are, let them alone; stay out of other people's affairs. Any place the spirits of the dead might be, they have their own work to do, and their own concerns to address; and we reserve no option to disrupt them. We can't help them, and it is exceptionally far-fetched whether they can help us, or whether we reserve any privilege to intrude upon their time on the off chance that they would be able. Leave the dead and the great beyond be, and tackle your own concern; get rich. Assuming that you start to blend in with the mysterious, you will begin mental cross-flows which will certainly carry your desires to wreck. Presently, this and the previous sections have carried us to the accompanying assertion of fundamental realities: There is reasoning stuff from which everything is made, and which, in its unique state, pervades, enters, and fills the interspaces of the universe. An idea, in this substance, creates what is imagined by the idea. Man can shape things in his idea, and, by presenting his thinking for undefined substance, can cause what he thinks is going to be made. To do this, man should pass from the serious to the imaginative brain; he should shape a reasonable mental image of the things he needs, and hold this image in his viewpoints with the decent Reason to get what he needs, and the resolute Confidence that he gets what he needs, shutting his psyche against all that might will generally shake his motivation, faint his vision, or extinguish his confidence. Furthermore, notwithstanding this, we will presently see that he should live and act with a particular goal in mind.

Chapter. 11

Acting with a particular goal in mind.

Believed is the imaginative influence, or the prompting force which makes the inventive influence act; figuring with a particular goal in mind will carry wealth to you, yet you should not depend upon thought alone, giving any consideration to an individual activity. That is the stone whereupon numerous generally logical otherworldly masterminds meet wreck - - the inability to associate ideas with individual activity. We have not yet arrived at the progressive phase, in any event, assuming such a phase to be conceivable, in what man can make straightforwardly from Shapeless Substance without nature's cycles or crafted by human hands; a man should think, yet his own activity should enhance his idea. By figuring you can prompt the gold in the hearts of the mountains to be actuated toward you; yet it won't mine itself, refine itself, coin itself into twofold hawks, and come moving along the streets looking for its way into your pocket. Under the inciting force of the Preeminent Soul, men's issues will be requested to the point that somebody will be directed to dig the gold for you; other men's deals will be coordinated to the point that the gold will be brought toward you, and you should so organize your own business undertakings that you might have the option to get it with regards to you. Your thinking makes all things, invigorating and lifeless, work to bring you what you need; however, your own movement should be with the end goal that you can appropriately get what you need when it contacts you. You are not to accept it as a good cause, nor to take it; you should give each man more worth than he gives you in real money esteem. The logical utilization of thought comprises framing an unmistakable and particular mental picture of what you need; clinging tightly to the reason to get what you need; and acknowledging with thankful confidence that you truly do get what you need. Try not to attempt to 'project' your thinking in any strange or mysterious manner, with having it go out and get things done for you; that

is squandered exertion, and will debilitate your ability to think with mental stability. The activity of thought in getting rich is completely made sense of in the first parts; your confidence and reason emphatically present your vision for Undefined Substance, which holds onto THE Very Longing FOR MORE LIFE THAT YOU HAVE; and this vision got from you, sets every one of the imaginative powers at work IN AND THROUGH THEIR Normal CHANNELS OF Activity, yet coordinated toward you. It isn't your part to direct or regulate the innovative approach; all you have to do with that is to hold your vision, adhere to your motivation, and keep up with your confidence and appreciation. However, you should act with a particular goal in mind, so you can fit what is yours with regards to you; so you can meet the things you have in your image and put them in their legitimate spots as they show up. You can truly see the reality of this. At the point when things contact you, they will be in the possession of different men, who will ask an identical for them. Also, you can get what is yours by giving the other man what is his. Your wallet won't be changed into a Fortunata's handbag, which will be in every case loaded with cash without exertion from you. This is the critical point in the study of getting rich; here, where thought and individual activity should be consolidated. There are a lot of individuals who, deliberately or unwittingly, set the imaginative powers in real life by the strength and steadiness of their cravings, however, they stay poor since they don't accommodate the gathering of what they need when it comes. By thought, what you need is brought to you; by the activity you get it. Anything your activity is to be, it is apparent that you should act NOW.

You can't act previously, and it is fundamental to the

clearness of your psychological vision that you excuse the past from your brain. You can't act in that frame of mind, for what's to come hasn't arrived at this point. What's more, you can't see how you will need to act in any future possibility until that possibility has shown up. Since you are not in the right business, or the right climate presently, don't imagine that you should delay activity until you get into the right business or climate. Also, don't invest energy in the current accepting idea with respect to the best course in inconceivable future crises; have confidence in your capacity to meet any crisis when it shows up. In the event that you act in the present with your psyche on the future, your current activity will accompany a separated brain, and won't be compelling. Put your entire brain into present activity. Try not to give your innovative drive to Unique Substance, and afterward plunk down and hang tight for results; on the off chance that you do, you won't ever get them. Act now. There will never be any time however presently, and there never will be any time yet presently. Assuming you are ever to start to prepare for the gathering of what you need, you should start now. What's more, your activity, anything that it is, should doubtlessly be in your current business or work and should be upon the people and things in your current climate. You can't act where you are not; you can't act where you have been, and you can't act where you will be; you can act just where you are. Try not to be annoyed about whether the previous work was all around good or poorly finished; accomplish today's worth of effort well. Try not to attempt to go about the upcoming responsibilities now; there will be a lot of opportunities to do that when you get to it. Try not to attempt, by mysterious or magical means, to follow up on individuals or things that are out of your compass. Try not to hang tight for a difference in climate, before you act; get a difference in climate by activity.

You can follow up on the climate in which you are currently, as to make yourself be moved to a superior climate. Hold with confidence and reason the vision of yourself in the better climate, yet follow up on your current climate with everything that is in you, energetically, and with all your brain. Invest no energy in wandering off in fantasy land or vision casting; hold to the one vision of what you need, and act NOW. Try not to project about looking for what should be done, or some peculiar, uncommon, or wonderful activity to proceed as an initial move toward getting rich. It is plausible that your activities, basically for quite a while to come, will be those you have been performing for quite a while past; yet you are to start now to play out these activities in the Specific Manner, which will without a doubt make you rich. Assuming you are participating in some business, and feel that it isn't the right one for you, don't hold on until you get into the right business before you start to act. Try not to feel deterred, or plunk down and regret since you are lost. No man was very lost except that he was unable to track down the ideal locations, and no man at any point turned out to be so engaged with some unacceptable business yet that he could get into the right business. Hold the vision of yourself in the right business, with the reason to get into it, and the confidence that you will get into it, and are getting into it; however ACT in your current business. Utilize your current business as the method for getting a superior one, and utilize your current climate as the method for getting into a superior one. Your vision of the right business, whenever held with confidence and reason, will make the Preeminent push the right business toward you; and your activity, in the event that acted in the Specific Way, will make you advance toward the business. Assuming you are a worker, or breadwinner, and feel that you should change puts in order to get what you need, don't project" your thinking into space and depend upon it to land you another position. It will likely neglect to do as such.

Hold the vision of yourself in the gig you need, while you ACT with confidence and reason hands on you have, and you will positively land the position you need. Your vision and confidence will get the imaginative power rolling to bring it toward you, and your activity will make the powers in your own current circumstance push you toward the spot you need. In closing this part, we will add one more explanation to our prospectus:- - There is reasoning stuff from which everything is made, and which, in its unique state, pervades, enters, and fills the interspaces of the universe. An idea, in this substance, creates what is imagined by the idea. Man can shape things in his idea, and, by presenting his thinking for nebulous substance, can cause what he thinks is going to be made. To do this, man should pass from the cutthroat to the imaginative psyche; he should shape an unmistakable mental image of the things he needs, and hold this image in his viewpoints with the decent Reason to get what he needs, and the steadfast Confidence that he gets what he needs, shutting his brain to all that might will generally shake his motivation, faint his vision, or extinguish his confidence. That he might get what he needs when it comes, man should act NOW upon individuals and things in his current climate.

Chapter.12

Productive Activity.

YOU should involve your thinking as coordinated in past parts, and start to give your best where you are, and you should give your best where you are. You can progress just by being bigger than your current spot, and no man is bigger than his current spot who leaves scattered any of the work relating to that spot. The world is progressed exclusively by individuals who more than fill their current spots. In the event that no man fills his current spot, you can see that there should be a move in reverse in all things. The people who don't exactly fill their current spots are extra weight upon society, government, trade, and industry; they should be conveyed along by others at an incredible cost. The advancement of the world is impeded exclusively by the individuals who don't fill the spots they are holding; they have a place with a previous age and a lower stage or plane of life, and their propensity is toward degeneration. No general public could progress assuming each man was more modest than his place; social advancement is directed by the law of physical and mental development. In the creature world, development is brought about by the abundance of life. At the point when an organic entity has more life than can be communicated in the elements of its own plane, it fosters the organs of a higher plane, and another species is started. There could never have been new species had there not been organic entities that more than filled their places. The law is the very same for you; getting rich relies on applying this rule to your own undertakings. Consistently is either an effective day or a day of disappointment, and it is the fruitful days that get you what you need. On the off chance that regular is a disappointment, you can never get rich; while in the event that consistently is a triumph, you can't neglect to get rich.

On the off chance that there is something that might be done today, and you don't make it happen, you have bombed to the extent that that thing is concerned, and the outcomes might be more tragic than you envision. You can't anticipate the aftereffects of even the most minor demonstration; you don't have the foggiest idea about the operations of the multitude of powers that have been set moving for your sake. Much might be relying upon your doing some basic demonstration; it could be the very thing which is to open the entryway of a chance to exceptionally incredible conceivable outcomes. You can never know every one of the mixes which Preeminent Insight is making for you in the realm of things and of human undertakings; your disregard or inability to do some little thing might create a long setback for getting what you need. Do, each day, Everything that could possibly be done that day. There is, nonetheless, a constraint or capability of the over that you should consider. You are not to exhaust, nor to rush aimlessly into your business in the work to do the best conceivable number of things in the briefest conceivable time. You are not to attempt to take care of the upcoming responsibilities today, nor to take care of seven days' responsibilities in a day. It is truly not the number of things you do, yet the Effectiveness of each different activity that matters. Each act is, in itself, either a triumph or a disappointment. Each act is, in itself, either powerful or wasteful. Each wasteful demonstration is a disappointment, and on the off chance that you go through your time on earth doing wasteful demonstrations, your entire life will be a disappointment. The more things you do, the more awful for you, on the off chance that every one of your demonstrations is wasteful. Then again, every productive demonstration is an outcome in itself, and in the event that each demonstration of your life is an effective one, your entire life Should be a triumph.

The reason for disappointment is doing an excessive number of things in a wasteful way, and not doing what's necessary for a proficient way. You will see that it is a plainly obvious recommendation that on the off chance that you do not wasteful demonstrations, and in the event that you do an adequate number of productive demonstrations, you will become rich. If, presently, it is workable for you to make each act a proficient one, you see again that the getting of wealth is decreased to an accurate science, similar to math. The matter turns, then, at that point, to the inquiry regarding whether you can make each different demonstration an outcome in itself. Furthermore, this you can absolutely do. You can make each act a triumph since ALL Power is working with you, and ALL Power can't come up short. Power is at your beck and call, and to make each act effective you have just to place power into it. Each activity is a major area of strength for either powerless; and when each one is solid, you are acting in the Specific Way which will make you rich. Each act can be a major area of strength made effective by holding your vision while you are making it happen, and putting the entire force of your Confidence and Reason into it. It is as of now that individuals bomb who separate mental power from individual activity. They utilize the force of the brain in one spot and at one time, and they act at another speed and at some other point. So their demonstrations are not effective in themselves; an excessive number of them are wasteful. Yet, in the event that ALL Power goes into each demonstration, regardless of how typical, each act will be an outcome in itself; and as in the idea of things each achievement opens the way to different victories, your advancement toward what you need, and the advancement of what you need toward you, will turn out to be progressively fast. Recollect that fruitful activity is aggregate in its outcomes. Since the longing for more life is intrinsic regardless, when a man starts to push toward a bigger life, more things connect themselves to him, and the impact of his craving is increased.

Do, each day, everything that could be done that day, and do each demonstration in an effective way. In saying that, you should hold your vision while you are doing each demonstration, but paltry or typical, I don't intend to say that it is essential consistently to see the vision unmistakably to its littlest subtleties. It ought to be crafted by your recreation hours to utilize your creative mind on the subtleties of your vision and to consider them until they are immovably fixed upon memory. Assuming you wish for fast outcomes, invest basically the entirety of your extra energy in this training. By consistent thought you will get the image of what you need, even to the littlest subtleties, so immovably fixed upon your brain, thus totally moved to the psyche of Undefined Substance, that in your functioning hours, you really want just to intellectually allude to the image to animate your confidence and reason and prompt your maximum effort to be advanced. Ponder your image in your recreation hours until your cognizance is so loaded with it that you can get a handle on it in a flash. You will turn out to be so enthused with its brilliant commitments that the simple idea of it will call forward the most grounded energies of your entire being. Allow us again to rehash our schedule, and by somewhat changing the end explanations carry it to the point we have now reached. There is reasoning stuff from which everything is made, and which, in its unique state, pervades, enters, and fills the interspaces of the universe. An idea, in this substance, creates what is imagined by the idea. Man can frame things in his idea, and, by presenting his thinking for undefined substance, can cause what he thinks is going to be made. To do this, man should pass from the serious to the imaginative psyche; he should shape an unmistakable mental image of the things he needs, and do, with confidence and reason, everything that could possibly be done every day, doing each different thing in an effective way.

Chapter. 13

Getting into the Right Business.

Achievement, in a specific business, depends for one thing upon your having in an advanced expression the resources expected in that business. Without a great melodic workforce, nobody can prevail as an educator of music; without advanced mechanical resources nobody can make extraordinary progress in any of the mechanical exchanges; without consideration and business resources, nobody can prevail in commercial pursuits. In any case, to have in advance express the resources expected in your specific job doesn't prevent you from getting rich. There are artists who have amazing abilities, and who still stay poor; there are metalworkers, woodworkers, etc who have magnificent mechanical capacity, but who don't get rich; and there are vendors with great resources for managing men who by the by come up short. The various resources are apparatuses; it is fundamental to have great devices, however, it is likewise fundamental that the instruments ought to be utilized in the Correct Manner. One man can take a sharp saw, a square, a decent plane, etc, and construct an attractive article of furniture; another man can take similar instruments and set to attempt to copy the article, however, his creation will be a mess up. He doesn't have the foggiest idea of how to involve great devices in a fruitful manner. The different resources of your psyche are the devices with which you should accomplish the work which is to make you rich; it will be more straightforward for you to succeed on the off chance that you get into a business for which you are exceptional with mental instruments. As a rule, will truly do best in that business which will utilize your most grounded resources; the one for which you are normally "best fitted." Yet there are constraints to this assertion, too. No man ought to see his business as being unalterably fixed by the propensities with which he was conceived. You can get wealthy in ANY business, for on the off chance that you do have not the right ability, you can foster that ability; it simply implies that you should make your apparatuses as you come, rather than binding

yourself to the utilization of those with which you were conceived. It will be more straightforward for you to prevail in a job for which you as of now have the gifts in an advanced state; however you CAN prevail in any work, for you can foster any simple ability, and there is no ability of which you have not basically the fundamentals. You will get rich most effectively, in truth, assuming you do that for which you are best fitted; yet you will get rich most acceptably if you do what you Like to do. Doing what you maintain that should do is life, and there is no genuine fulfillment in living assuming we are constrained to be always accomplishing something which we could do without doing, and can never do what we like to do. Also, it is sure that you can do what you like to do; the craving to do it is confirmation that you have inside you the power which can make it happen. Want is a sign of force. The longing to play music is the power that can play music looking for articulation and improvement; the craving to create mechanical gadgets is the mechanical ability looking for articulation and advancement. Where there is no power, either created or lacking, to do a thing, there will never be any longing to do that thing; and where there is a powerful urge to do a thing, it is sure evidence that the ability to do it is solid, and just expects to be created and applied in the Correct Manner. All things being equal, it is ideal to choose the business for which you have the best-developed ability; yet on the off chance that you genuinely want to participate in a specific profession, you ought to choose that work as a definitive end at which you point. You can do what you like to do, and it is your right and honor to follow the business or diversion which will be generally harmonious and lovely. You are not obliged to do what you could do without to do, and shouldn't do it besides as a way to carry you to the doing of what you need to do.

Assuming there are previous slip-ups whose outcomes have put you in an unfortunate business or climate, you might be obliged for quite a while to do what you could do without to do; however, you can make the doing of it charming by realizing that it is making it feasible for you to come to the doing of what you need to do. In the event that you feel that you are not in the right work, don't act excessively quickly in attempting to get into another. The most effective way, by and large, to change business or climate is by development. Don't hesitate for even a moment to make an unexpected and extremist change in the event that the open door is introduced, and assuming you feel after conscious thought that it is the ideal open door; yet never make an abrupt or revolutionary move when you are in uncertainty with respect to the insight of doing as such. There will never be any rush on the inventive plane, and there is no absence of chance. At the point when you escape the serious psyche you won't comprehend that you ever need to quickly act. No other person will beat you to what you need to do; there is enough for all. On the off chance that one space is taken, one more and a superior one will be opened for you somewhat farther on; there is a lot of time. At the point when you are in uncertainty, stand by. Back up on the thought of your vision, increment your confidence and reason; and definitely, in the midst of uncertainty and hesitation, develop appreciation. A little while spent pondering the vision of what you need, and decisively thanksgiving that you are getting it, will bring your brain into a such cozy relationship with the Preeminent that you will commit no error when you do act. There is a psyche that realizes everything to be aware of; and you can come into close solidarity with this brain leaning on an unshakable conviction and the reason to progress throughout everyday life, on the off chance that you have profound appreciation. Botches come from acting quickly, or from acting in dread or uncertainty, or in absent-mindedness of the Right Rationale, which is more life to all, and less to none.

As you happen in the Specific Manner, open doors will come to you in expanding numbers; and you should be exceptionally consistent in your confidence and reason, and keep in close touch with the All Psyche with respectful appreciation. Give your very best in an ideal way consistently, yet do it without scramble, stress, or dread. Go as quickly as possible, yet never rush. Recall that at the time you start to hustle, you fail to be a maker and turn into a contender; you drop back upon the old plane once more. Whenever you regard yourself as rushing, call an end; fix your consideration on the psychological picture of what you need, and start to express gratefulness that you are getting it. The activity of Appreciation won't ever neglect to fortify your confidence and reestablish your motivation.

Chapter.14

The Impression of Increment.

Regardless of whether you change your work, your activities for the present should be those relating to the business in which you are currently locked. You can get into the business you need by utilizing the business you are now settled in; by taking care of your everyday responsibilities with a particular goal in mind. Furthermore, to the extent that your business comprises managing different men, whether actually or by letter, the key thought about the entirety of your endeavors should be to pass on to their psyches the impression of increment. The increment is what all men and all ladies are looking for; it is the inclination of the Amorphous Insight inside them, looking for more full articulation. The craving for an increment is innate in all nature; it is the major motivation of the universe. All human exercises depend on the craving for increment; individuals are looking for more food, more garments, better asylum, more extravagance, more magnificence, more information, more delight - - expansion in something, more life. Each residing thing is under this need for consistent progression; where the increment of life stops, disintegration and demise set in without a moment's delay. Man intuitively knows this, and subsequently, he is perpetually looking for more. This law of unending increment is gone ahead by Jesus in the story of the gifts; just the people who acquire hold any; from him who hath not will be removed even what he hath. The typical craving for expanded abundance is definitely not malevolent or something inexcusable; it is essentially the longing for a more plentiful life; it is yearning.

Furthermore, on the grounds that it is the most profound impulse of their tendencies, all people are drawn to him who can give them a greater amount of the method for life. In following the Specific Manner as depicted in the previous pages, you are getting non stop increments for yourself, and you are giving it to all with whom you bargain. You are an inventive focus, from which increment is radiated to all. Make certain of this, and pass affirmation of the reality on to everyone with whom you come in touch. Regardless of how little the exchange, regardless of whether it be just the offering of a stick of treats to a small kid, put into it the possibility of increment, and ensure that the client is dazzled with the idea. Convey the impression of progression with all that you do, so that all individuals will get the feeling that you are a Propelling Individual, and that you advance all who manage you. Indeed, even to individuals whom you meet in a social manner, with next to no considered business, and to whom you don't attempt to sell anything, give the possibility of increment. You can convey this impression by holding the relentless confidence that you, yourself, are obstructing Increment; and by allowing this confidence to rouse, fill, and penetrate each activity. Do all that you do with the firm feeling that you are a propelling character and that you are giving headway to everyone. Feel that you are getting rich and that in this manner you are making others rich, and presenting benefits to all. Try not to flaunt or gloat about your prosperity, or discuss it superfluously; genuine confidence is rarely pretentious. Any place you find an egoistic individual, you find one who is furtively far-fetched and apprehensive. Basically feel the confidence, and let it sort out in each exchange; let each demonstration and tone and look express the tranquil affirmation that you are getting rich; that you are as of now rich. Words won't be important to impart

this inclination to other people; they will feel the feeling of increment when in your presence, and will be drawn to you in the future. You should dazzle others so that they will feel that in partnership with you, they will get an increment for themselves. See that you give them a utilization esteem more prominent than the money esteem you are taking from them. Take genuine pride in doing this, and let everyone in on it, and you will have no absence of clients. Individuals will go where they are given increment; and the Preeminent, which wants expansion altogether, and which knows all, will push toward you people who have never known about you. Your business will expand quickly, and you will be astounded at the surprising advantages which will come to you. You will be capable from one day to another to make bigger blends, securing more prominent benefits, and to happen into a more harmonious job in the event that you want to do such. However, in doing this, you should never neglect to focus on your vision of what you need, or your confidence and reason to get what you need. Let me here provide you with one more fair warning concerning intentions. Be careful with the guileful impulse to look for control over different men. Nothing is so wonderful to the unformed or somewhat created mind as the activity of force or territory over others. The longing to govern for egotistical satisfaction has been the scourge of the world. For endless ages rulers and masters have soaked the earth with blood in their fights to broaden their territories; this is not to look for more life for all, but rather to get more power for themselves. Today, the principal rationale in the business and modern world is something very similar; men marshal their multitudes of dollars and ruin the lives and hearts of millions in a similar distraught scramble for control over others. Business lords, as political rulers, are propelled by the desire for power.

Jesus found in this longing for authority the moving motivation of that detestable world He tried to oust. Peruse the twenty-third part of Matthew, and perceive how He pictures the desire of the Pharisees to be designated "Expert," to sit in the high places, to domineer over others, and to lay troubles on the backs of the less lucky; and note how He contrasts this desire for territory and the kindly looking for the Benefit of all to which He calls His followers. Pay special attention to the compulsion to look for power, to turn into an "ace," to be considered as one who is above the normal crowd, to intrigue others by extravagant presentation, etc. The brain that looks for dominance over others is the cutthroat psyche, and the serious psyche isn't the inventive one. To dominate your current circumstance and your predetermination, it isn't by any stretch important that you ought to manage over your kindred men, and without a doubt, when you fall into the world's battle for the high places, you start to be vanquished by destiny and climate, and your getting rich turns into an issue of possibility and hypothesis. Be careful with the cutthroat psyche!! No better assertion of the guideline of innovative activity can be figured out than the most loved announcement of the late "Brilliant Rule" Jones of Toledo: "What I need for myself, I need for everyone.

Chapter 15

The Propelling Man.

What I have said in the last part applies too to the expert man and the worker regarding the one who is taking part in the trade business. Regardless of whether you are a doctor, an instructor, or a priest, in the event that you can give an increment of life to other people and make them reasonable in reality, they will be drawn to you, and you will get rich. The doctor who holds the vision of himself as an extraordinary and fruitful healer, and who pursues the total acknowledgment of that vision with confidence and reason, as portrayed in previous sections, will come into such close touch with the Wellspring of Life that he will find true success; patients will come to him in crowds. Nobody has a more prominent chance to convey the impact of the educating of this book than the specialist of medication; it doesn't make any difference to which of the different schools he might have a place, for the guideline of recuperating is normal to everyone of them, and might be reached by all indistinguishable. The Propelling Man in medication, who holds to a reasonable mental picture of himself as effective, and who submits to the honest laws, reason, and appreciation, will fix each treatable case he embraces, regardless of what cures he might utilize. In the field of religion, the world shouts out for the priest who can show his listeners the genuine study of bountiful life. He who aces the subtleties of the study of getting rich, along with the partnered studies of being great, of being perfect, and of winning affection, and who shows these subtleties from the platform, won't ever need for a gathering. This is the gospel that the world requires; it will give an increment of life, and men will hear it readily and will give liberal help to the one who carries it to them. What is presently required is an exhibition of the study of life from the platform. We need evangelists who can let us know how, yet who in their own people will show us how.

We want an evangelist who will be rich, sound, extraordinary, and

darling, to show us how to accomplish these things, and when he comes he will see us as a various and faithful following. The equivalent is valid for the educator who can motivate the kids with confidence and reason for propelling life. He won't ever be "out of a task." And any instructor who has this confidence and reason can give it to his students; he can't resist the urge to give it to them in the event that it is essential for his own life and practice. What is valid for the instructor, minister, and doctor is valid for the attorney, dental specialist, landman, protection specialist - - of everyone. The joint mental and individual activity I have depicted is dependable; it can't fizzle. Each man and lady who adheres to these directions consistently, perseveringly, and exactly, will get rich. The law of the Increment of Life is as numerically sure in its activity as the law of attraction; getting rich is a definite science. The breadwinner will track down this as valid for his case as of any of the others referenced. Try not to feel that you get no opportunity to get rich since you are working where there is no apparent chance for headway, where wages are little, and the cost for most everyday items is high. Structure your unmistakable mental vision of what you need, and start to act with confidence and reason. Accomplish basically everything you can do, consistently, and do each piece of work in a completely effective way; put the influence of progress, and the reason to get rich, into all that you do. Yet, don't do this just by currying favor with your manager, with the expectation that he, or those above you, will see your great work and advance you; it isn't possible that they will do as such. The one who is just a "great" worker, filling his place to the absolute best of his capacity, and happy with that, is important to his manager; and it isn't to the business' advantage to advance him; he is worth more where he is. To get progression, something more is fundamental than to be excessively enormous for your place.

The individual who is sure to progress is the person who is too large for his place, and who has an unmistakable idea of what he needs to be; who can say for sure that he can become what he needs to be and not entirely set in stone to BE what he needs to be. Try not to attempt to more than fill your current spot more with the end goal of satisfying your manager; do it by propelling yourself. Hold the confidence and motivation behind increment during work hours, after work hours, and before work hours. Hold it so that each individual who interacts with you, whether foreman, individual laborer, or social associate, will feel the force of direction transmitting from you; so everyone will get the feeling of headway and increment from you. Men will be drawn to you, and on the off chance that there are no opportunities for headway in your current work, you will very soon see a chance to take another job. There is a Power that never neglects to introduce an open door to the Propelling Man who is moving in compliance with the regulation. God can't resist the urge to help you, in the event that you act with a specific goal in mind; He should do as such to help Himself. There isn't anything in your conditions or in the modern circumstance that can hold you down. In the event that you can't get rich working for the steel trust, you can get rich on a ten-section of the land ranch; and assuming you start to move in the Specific Manner, you will positively escape from the "grasp" of the steel trust and get on to the homestead or any place else you wish to be. In the event that two or three of a huge number of its representatives would enter upon the Specific Way, the steel trust would before long be in a terrible predicament; it would need to offer its working men more chances or leave the business. No one needs to work for a trust; the trusts can keep men in supposed sad circumstances just inasmuch as there are men who are too oblivious to even consider knowing about the study of getting rich, or excessively mentally lethargic to rehearse it. Start this perspective and acting, and your confidence and reason will make you speedy to see an amazing open door to better your condition.

Such open doors will expediently come, for the Preeminent, working all together, and working for you, will bring them before you. Try not to hang tight for a potential chance to be all that you need to be; the point at which a valuable chance to be more than you are currently is introduced and you feel affected toward it, take it. It will be the most vital move toward a more prominent open door. There is no such thing conceivable in this universe as an absence of chances for the one who is carrying on with the propelling life. It is innate in the constitution of the universe that all things will be for himself and turn out together for his great, and he should unquestionably get rich assuming he acts and thinks in the Specific Manner. So let working-class people concentrate on this book with incredible consideration, and enter with certainty upon the strategy it endorses; it won't come up short.

Chapter. 16

A few Alerts, and Closing Perceptions.

MANY individuals will laugh at the possibility that there is a precise study of getting rich; holding the feeling that the stockpile of abundance is restricted, they will demand that social and legislative organizations should be changed before even any impressive number of individuals can procure a capability. Be that as it may, this isn't accurate. The facts confirm that current states keep the majority in neediness, yet this is on the grounds that the majority don't think and act in the Specific Manner. In the event that the majority start to push ahead as proposed in this book, neither legislatures nor modern frameworks can really take a look at them; all frameworks should be changed to oblige the positive headway. Assuming individuals have the Propelling Brain, have the Confidence that they can become rich, and push ahead with a decent reason to become rich, nothing might perhaps keep them in destitution. People might enter upon the Specific Way whenever, and under any administration, and make themselves rich; and when any extensive number of people do as such under any administration, they will make the framework be so adjusted as to open the way for other people. The more individuals who get rich on the serious plane, the more terrible for other people; the more who get rich on the imaginative plane, the better for other people. The financial salvation of the majority must be achieved by getting an enormous number of individuals to rehearse the logical technique put down in this book and become rich. These will show others the way, and motivate them with a craving for reality, with the confidence that it very well may be accomplished, and with the reason to achieve it.

For the present, in any case, it is sufficient to realize that neither the public authority under which you live nor the free enterprise or cutthroat arrangement of an industry can hold you back from getting rich. At the point when you enter upon the innovative plane of figure you will transcend everything and become a resident of another realm. However, recall that your thinking should be held upon the innovative plane; you are never for a moment to be double-crossed into viewing the inventory as restricted, or into following up on the ethical degree of the contest. Whenever you truly do fall into old methods of thought, right yourself in a split second; for when you are in the serious psyche, you have lost the participation of the Brain of the Entirety. Invest no energy in arranging respect to how you will meet potential crises from here on out, besides the essential strategies that might influence your activities today. You are worried about taking care of the present responsibilities in an entirely effective way, and not with crises that might emerge tomorrow; you can take care of them. Try not to fret about questions regarding how you will conquer impediments that might linger upon your business skyline, except if you can see obviously that your course should be changed today to keep away from them. Regardless of how gigantic an impediment might show up a ways off, you will see that on the off chance that you happen in the Specific Manner, it will vanish as you approach it, or that a way finished, however, or around it will show up. No conceivable blend of conditions can overcome a man or lady who is continuing to get rich along rigorously logical lines. No man or lady who submits to the law can neglect to get rich, anything other than one can increase in pairs and neglect to get four. Give no genuine concern to potential catastrophes, hindrances, panics, or ominous mixes of conditions; it is time to the point of meeting such things when they introduce themselves before you in the quick present, and you will find that each trouble conveys with it the fortitude for its surviving.

Watch your discourse. Never discuss yourself, your issues, or whatever else in a deterred or beating way down. Never concede the chance of disappointment, or talk such that derives disappointment as a chance. Never talk about the times as being hard, or of business conditions as being dubious. Times might be hard and business dubious for individuals who are on a serious plane, yet they can never be so for you; you can make what you need, and you are above dread. At the point when others are having tough situations and unfortunate business, you will track down your most prominent open doors. Train yourself to consider and to view the world as something which is Becoming, which is developing; and to see what appears to be underhanded as being just that which is lacking. Continuously talk regarding progression; to do in any case is to deny your confidence, and to deny your confidence is to lose it. Never permit yourself to feel disheartened. You might hope to have something specific at a specific time, and not get it around then, and this will appear to you as a disappointment. Yet, assuming you hold to your confidence you will observe that the disappointment is just evident. Happen in a specific manner, and on the off chance that you don't get that thing, you will get something such a ton better that you will see that the appearing disappointment was actually an extraordinary achievement. An understudy of this science had focused on making a specific business blend that appeared to him as an opportunity to be entirely alluring, and he worked for certain weeks to achieve it. At the point when the vital opportunity arrived, the thing flopped in a totally mysterious way; maybe some concealed impact had been working furtively against him. He was not disheartened; going against the norm, he said thanks to God that his craving had been overruled, and went consistently on with an appreciative psyche. In half a month an open door such a ton better came to his direction that he could not have possibly made the main arrangement regardless; and he saw that a Brain

which realized more than he knew had kept him from losing everyone's benefit by catching himself with the lesser. That is the manner in which each appearing disappointment will turn out for you, assuming you keep your confidence, hold to your motivation, have an appreciation, and do, each day, everything that could possibly be done that day, doing each different demonstration in a fruitful way. The point when you make disappointment is on the grounds that you have not requested enough; keep on, and something bigger than you were looking for will positively come to you. Recollect this. You won't fizzle since you come up short on the vital ability to do what you wish to do. On the off chance that you happen as I have guided, you will foster all the abilities that are important to the accomplishment of your work. It isn't inside the extent of this book to manage the study of developing ability; however, it is essentially as certain and straightforward as the method involved with getting rich. In any case, don't hold back or falter for dread that when you come to a specific spot you will fall flat for the absence of capacity; keep right on, and when you come to that spot, the capacity will be outfitted to you. A similar wellspring of Capacity that empowered the unschooled Lincoln to accomplish the best work in government at any point achieved by a solitary man is available to you; you might draw upon all the psyche it is for shrewdness to use in gathering the obligations which are laid upon you. Happen in full confidence. Concentrate on this book. Cause it your steady friend until you have dominated every one of the thoughts contained in it. While you are getting solidly settled in this confidence, you will in all actuality do well to surrender most entertainments and delight; and to avoid spots where thoughts clashing with these are progressed in talks or lessons. Try not to peruse critical or clashing writing, or get into contentions upon the matter. Do next to no perusing, beyond the scholars referenced in the Prelude. Invest the greater part of your relaxation energy in considering your vision, developing appreciation, and pursuing this book. It contains all you want to know about the study of getting rich, and you will find every one of the fundamentals summarized in the accompanying part.

Outline of the Study of Getting Rich.

There is reasoning stuff from which everything is made, and which, in its unique state, pervades, enters, and fills the interspaces of the universe. An idea in this substance delivers what is imagined by the idea. Man can shape things in his idea, and putting forth his thinking for nebulous substances can cause what he thinks is going to be made. To do this, man should pass from the cutthroat to the imaginative psyche; if not he can't be as one with the Amorphous Knowledge, which is consistently innovative and never aggressive in the soul. The man might come into full congruity with the Undefined Substance by engaging an exuberant and earnest appreciation for the favors it presents to him. Appreciation brings together the psyche of a man with the mental fortitude of Substance, so that man's contemplations are gotten by the Amorphous. Man can stay upon the inventive plane simply by joining himself with the Indistinct Knowledge through a profound and constant sensation of appreciation. The man should frame a reasonable and distinct mental picture of the things he wishes to have, to do, or to become; and he should hold this psychological picture in his viewpoints while being profoundly thankful to the Preeminent that every one of his longings is conceded to him. The one who wishes to get rich should spend his relaxation hours thinking about his Vision, and decisively thanksgiving that the fact of the matter is being given to him. An excessive amount of pressure can't be laid on the significance of incessant examination of the psychological picture, combined with relentless confidence and passionate appreciation. This is the cycle by which the impression is given to the Shapeless, and the imaginative powers put into high gear. The inventive energy deals with the laid-out channels of normal development, and modern and social requests. All that is

I remembered for his psychological picture will most likely be brought to the one who adheres to the directions given above, and whose confidence doesn't falter. What he needs will come to him through the methods of laid-out exchange and trade. To accept his own when it will come to him, man should be dynamic, and this movement can comprise more than filling his current spot. He should remember the Reason to help the rich through the acknowledgment of his psychological picture. What's more, he should do, each day, everything that could possibly be done that day, taking consideration to do each demonstration in a fruitful way. He should provide for each man utilization esteem in overabundance of the money esteem he gets, so every exchange makes for more life, and he should hold the Propelling Idea that the impression of increment will be conveyed to all with whom he comes in touch. The people who practice the previous guidelines will surely get rich; and the wealth they get will be in precise extent to the definiteness of their vision, the fixity of their motivation, the relentlessness of their confidence, and the profundity of their appreciation.